THE LIFE OF
SALLY RIDE

BY ELIZABETH RAUM

AMICUS | AMICUS INK

Sequence is published by Amicus and Amicus Ink
P.O. Box 1329, Mankato, MN 56002
www.amicuspublishing.us

Library of Congress Cataloging-in-Publication Data
Names: Raum, Elizabeth, author.
Title: The Life of Sally Ride / by Elizabeth Raum.
Description: Mankato, Minnesota : Amicus, [2019] | Series: Sequence | Series: Change maker biographies | Includes bibliographical references and index.
Identifiers: LCCN 2018027512 (print) | LCCN 2018029154 (ebook) | ISBN 9781681517629 (pdf) | ISBN 9781681516806 (library binding : alk. paper) | ISBN 9781681524665 (pbk. : alk. paper)
Subjects: LCSH: Ride, Sally--Juvenile literature. | Women astronauts--United States Biography--Juvenile literature. | Astronauts--United States--Biography--Juvenile literature.
Classification: LCC TL789.85.R53 (ebook) | LCC TL789.85.R53 R383 2019 (print) | DDC 629.450092 [B] --dc23
LC record available at https://lccn.loc.gov/2018027512

Editor: Alissa Thielges
Designer: Ciara Beitlich
Photo Researcher: Holly Young

Acknowledgement: Many thanks to Tam O'Shaughnessy for her assistance in providing photographs and reviewing this book before publication.

Photo Credits: Alamy/NASA Photo cover; NASA 5, 14–15, 16–17, 24–25, 28–29; Tam/Courtesy of Tam O'Shaughnessy 6; Alamy/Aviation History Collection 8–9; Getty/Bettmann 10–11; AP/ASSOCIATED PRESS 13; AP/Bruce Weaver 18; AP/Bob Daugherty 20; AP/Gerald Herbert 23; Newscom/Reuters/Charles W. Luzier 27; AP/USPS 28

HC 10 9 8 7 6 5 4 3 2 1
PB 10 9 8 7 6 5 4 3 2 1

TABLE OF CONTENTS

Who was Sally Ride?

In 1983, Sally Ride flew into space on a **space shuttle**. It was a big moment in American history. She was the first U.S. woman in space. At age 32, she was also the youngest American in space. Sally didn't always dream of being an astronaut. But her journey into space inspired many others. She paved the way for women and girls to follow.

LOADING . . . LOADING . . . LOADING . . .

This is Sally Ride's official **NASA** picture. It was taken after her first space flight.

Sally, age 10, practices tennis.

Sally Ride is born.

LOADING...LOADING...

Choosing Science

Sally Kristen Ride was born on May 26, 1951, in Los Angeles, California. Sally loved sports. Her parents sent her to tennis lessons. Soon, she was winning matches. She earned a tennis **scholarship** to high school. In college, she decided to stop competing in tennis. She focused on science instead.

At the time, few women studied science. That didn't stop Sally Ride. She studied **physics**, the science of matter and energy. She planned to teach college. Then in 1977, Sally saw an article in the student newspaper. It said, "NASA to **recruit** women." Earlier astronauts were all men.

Sally studies to finish her PhD in physics.

Sally Ride is born.

MAY 26, 1951   1977

ING . . . LOADING . . .

NASA advertises for women astronauts.

LOADING...LOADING...LOADING...

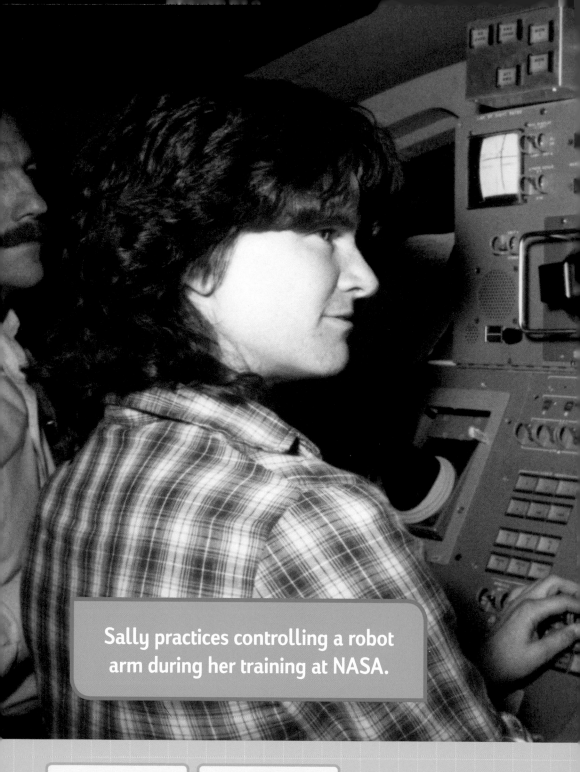

Sally practices controlling a robot arm during her training at NASA.

Sally Ride is born.

Sally begins astronaut training.

MAY 26, 1951   1977   AUGUST 1978

LOADING...

NASA advertises for women astronauts.

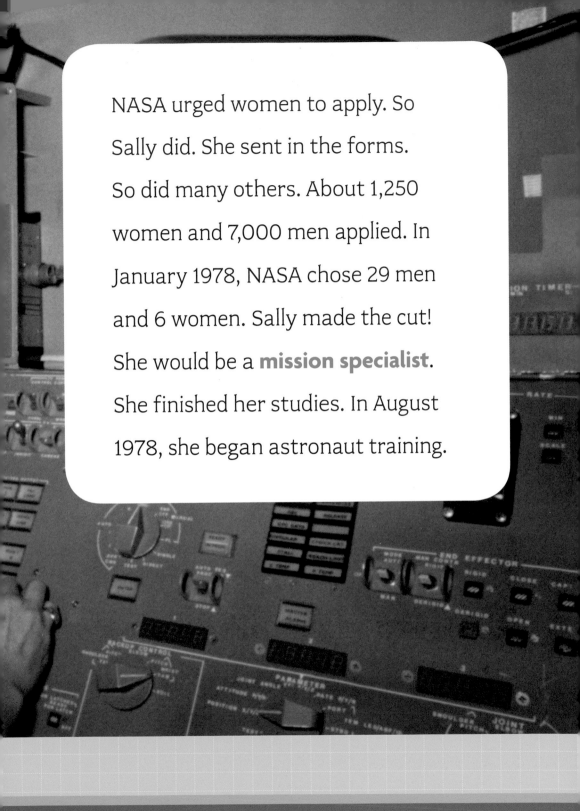

NASA urged women to apply. So Sally did. She sent in the forms. So did many others. About 1,250 women and 7,000 men applied. In January 1978, NASA chose 29 men and 6 women. Sally made the cut! She would be a **mission specialist**. She finished her studies. In August 1978, she began astronaut training.

LOADING... LOADING... LOADING...

Into Space

Sally learned all about the space shuttle and its life-support system. She practiced being weightless. She helped design a robot arm. She even learned to fly a plane. On June 18, 1983, Sally soared into space. It was NASA's first mission with a **crew** of five people. A crowd of 250,000 watched the liftoff. Many yelled, "Ride, Sally Ride!"

Sally Ride is born.

Sally begins astronaut training.

MAY 26, 1951   1977   AUGUST 1978   JUNE 18, 1983   ADING . . .

NASA advertises for women astronauts.

Sally is the first U.S. woman in space.

Ready for takeoff! The crew waves to the crowd as they walk to the shuttle.

Sally Ride is born.

Sally begins astronaut training.

Sally returns to Earth.

MAY 26, 1951   1977   AUGUST 1978   JUNE 18, 1983   JUNE 24, 1983

NASA advertises for women astronauts.

Sally is the first U.S. woman in space.

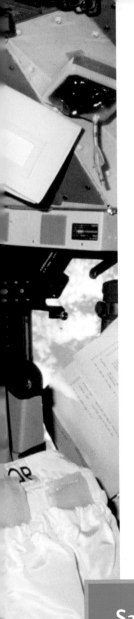

Sally Ride spent a total of 147 hours in space. Over the six days, the crew did many experiments. As a mission specialist, Sally studied how some metals mixed together. She also used the robot arm to lift two **satellites** into **orbit**. The crew returned to Earth on June 24.

Sally floats around and talks with NASA back on Earth.

LOADING . . . LOADING . . . LOADING . . .

On October 5, 1984, Sally flew into space again. She was part of NASA's biggest crew yet. Of the seven people, two were women. The mission lasted eight days. Sally used two TV cameras and a big still camera to take pictures of Earth. With the shuttle's robot arm, she put another satellite into orbit. It measured the sun's energy.

Sally used a robot arm to launch this satellite into orbit.

Sally Ride is born.

Sally begins astronaut training.

Sally returns to Earth.

MAY 26, 1951   1977   AUGUST 1978   JUNE 18, 1983   JUNE 24, 1983   OCTOBER 5, 1984

NASA advertises for women astronauts.

Sally is the first U.S. woman in space.

Sally takes second space flight.

The *Challenger* exploded 73 seconds into its flight. Many people watched on TV.

Sally Ride is born.

Sally begins astronaut training.

Sally returns to Earth.

MAY 26, 1951   1977   AUGUST 1978   JUNE 18, 1983   JUNE 24, 1983   OCTOBER 5, 1984

NASA advertises for women astronauts.

Sally is the first U.S. woman in space.

Sally takes second space flight.

Making Space Flights Safer

Sally was training for a third space flight. But on a cold morning, January 28, 1986, the space shuttle *Challenger* blew up during takeoff. All seven astronauts died. NASA put all flights on hold. President Ronald Reagan asked Sally to help study the accident. Sally agreed. She was on a team with 14 other people. They were all experts in their fields.

Space shuttle *Challenger* explodes; Sally studies cause.

1986

LOADING... LOADING...

Sally Ride is born.		Sally begins astronaut training.		Sally returns to Earth.		
MAY 26, 1951	1977	AUGUST 1978	JUNE 18, 1983	JUNE 24, 1983	OCTOBER 5, 1984	
	NASA advertises for women astronauts.		Sally is the first U.S. woman in space.		Sally takes second space flight.	

Sally asked hard questions. Her team found that the shuttle's O-rings caused the explosion. O-rings are rubber seals. Cold weather made them fail. An engineer had told NASA to delay the launch. But delays cost money. So NASA refused. Sally said safety must come first. In 1987, Sally retired from NASA.

Sally took part in the case hearings. She reported her team's findings.

Space shuttle *Challenger* explodes; Sally studies cause.

1986   1987   DING . . . LOADING . . .

Sally retires from NASA.

Encouraging Others

After retiring, Sally taught physics in college and did research. In 1989, she co-wrote a children's book with Susan Okie, *To Space and Back*. It talks about her space flights. She co-wrote seven more books for kids with Tam O'Shaughnessy. Seeing Earth from space made Sally care about the **environment**. Sally and Tam wrote *Mission: Planet Earth*. It talks about Earth's changing climate.

Sally Ride is born.	Sally begins astronaut training.		Sally returns to Earth.	

MAY 26, 1951	1977	AUGUST 1978	JUNE 18, 1983	JUNE 24, 1983	OCTOBER 5, 1984

	NASA advertises for women astronauts.		Sally is the first U.S. woman in space.		Sally takes second space flight.

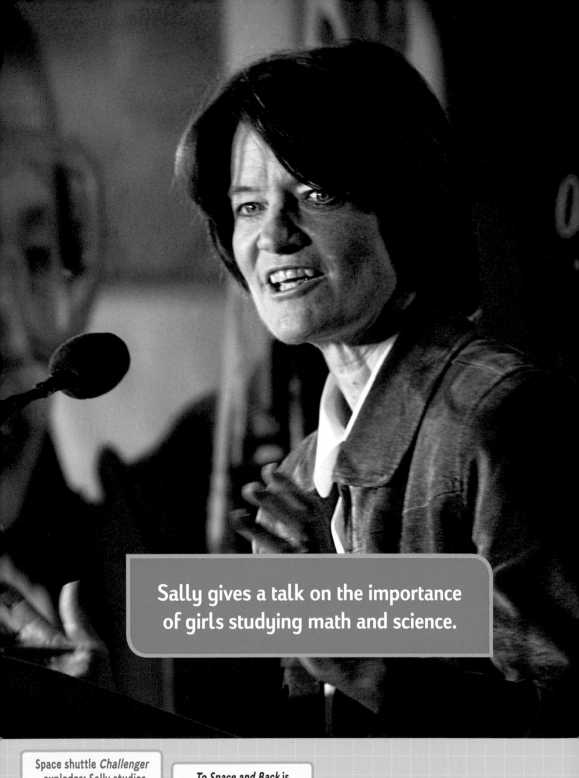

Sally gives a talk on the importance of girls studying math and science.

Space shuttle *Challenger* explodes; Sally studies cause.

To Space and Back is published.

1986   1987   1989

Sally retires from NASA.

. . . L O A D I N G . . .

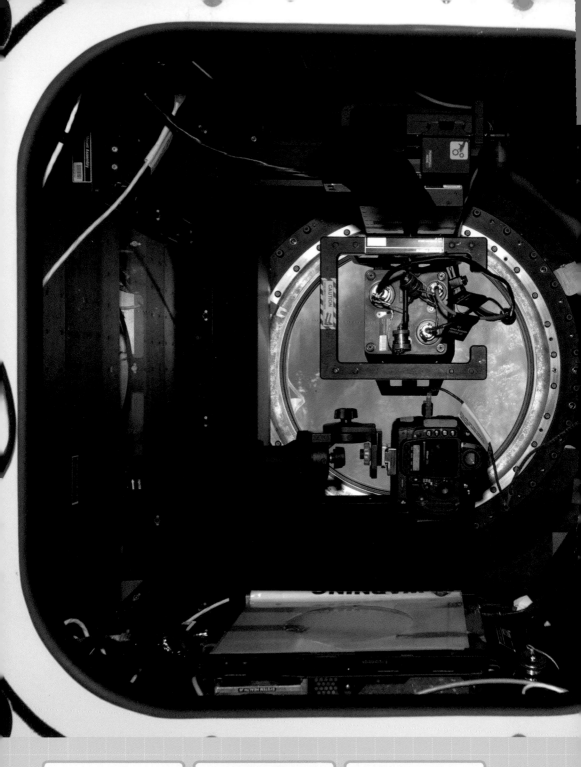

Sally Ride is born.

Sally begins astronaut training.

Sally returns to Earth.

MAY 26, 1951   1977   AUGUST 1978   JUNE 18, 1983   JUNE 24, 1983   OCTOBER 5, 1984

NASA advertises for women astronauts.

Sally is the first U.S. woman in space.

Sally takes second space flight.

In 2001, Sally started a company with Tam and some other friends. It's called Sally Ride Science. Its programs encourage kids to study science. Sally wanted to "make science and engineering cool again." She also worked with NASA to set up the Sally Ride EarthKAM. This camera orbits Earth on the International Space Station. Kids can use it to take pictures of the Earth from space.

The EarthKAM looks down at Earth. This is the view inside it.

Space shuttle *Challenger* explodes; Sally studies cause.

To Space and Back is published.

| 1986 | 1987 | 1989 | 2001 |

Sally retires from NASA.

Sally Ride Science programs begin.

ꓷADING...

Sally Ride was well respected as both a scientist and an astronaut. When the *Columbia* shuttle broke apart on February 1, 2003, NASA asked Sally to study the cause. She was the only astronaut to help **investigate** both shuttle accidents.

In June, Sally was **inducted** into the Astronaut Hall of Fame. She was the first woman to receive that honor.

Sally smiles at the Hall of Fame ceremony.

Sally Ride is born.	Sally begins astronaut training.	Sally returns to Earth.
MAY 26, 1951	1977 AUGUST 1978 JUNE 18, 1983 JUNE 24, 1983 OCTOBER 5, 1984	
	NASA advertises for women astronauts.	Sally is the first U.S. woman in space. Sally takes second space flight.

Space shuttle *Challenger* explodes; Sally studies cause.

To Space and Back is published.

Sally investigates *Columbia* accident; inducted into Astronaut Hall of Fame.

1986   1987   1989   2001   2003

Sally retires from NASA.

Sally Ride Science programs begin.

Sally Ride is born.

Sally begins astronaut training.

Sally returns to Earth.

MAY 26, 1951   1977   AUGUST 1978   JUNE 18, 1983   JUNE 24, 1983   OCTOBER 5, 1984

NASA advertises for women astronauts.

Sally is the first U.S. woman in space.

Sally takes second space flight.

Sally Ride died of cancer in 2012. In 2013, President Barack Obama awarded her the Presidential Medal of Freedom. He said, "Sally's life showed us that there are no limits to what we can achieve." In 2018, more than one-fourth of NASA astronauts were women. Sally Ride led the way.

In 2018, a Sally Ride stamp was made. It honors her life.

Space shuttle *Challenger* explodes; Sally studies cause.		*To Space and Back* is published.		Sally investigates *Columbia* accident; inducted into Astronaut Hall of Fame.	
1986	1987	1989	2001	2003	JULY 23, 2012
	Sally retires from NASA.		Sally Ride Science programs begin.		Sally Ride dies of cancer.

Glossary

crew A team of people who work together on a job.

environment The natural world of land, sea, and air.

induct To officially welcome someone as a member of a group or organization.

investigate To study or examine in detail.

mission specialist An astronaut crew member who performs scientific, medical, or engineering experiments in space.

NASA National Aeronautics and Space Administration; the federal agency that carries out work in space.

orbit A circular path an object makes around a planet, star, or moon.

physics The science that studies matter and energy, including light, heat, sound, electricity, motion, and force.

recruit To get someone to join a group.

satellite A device sent into orbit, often for communication purposes.

scholarship Money given to a student to help pay for schooling.

space shuttle A vehicle designed to carry astronauts into space and back.

Read More

Anderson, AnnMarie. *Sally Ride.* New York: Scholastic, 2015.

Goldstein, Margaret J. *Astronaut and Physicist Sally Ride.* Minneapolis, Minn.: Lerner, 2018.

Loh-Hagan, Virginia. *Sally Ride.* Ann Arbor, Mich.: Cherry Lake Publishing, 2018.

O'Shaughnessy, Tam. *Sally Ride: A Photobiography of America's Pioneering Woman in Space.* New York: Roaring Brook Press, 2015.

Websites

NASA | Who Was Sally Ride?
https://www.nasa.gov/audience/forstudents/k-4/stories/nasa-knows/who-was-sally-ride-k4.html

Sally Ride EarthKam
https://www.earthkam.org/

Sally Ride Science
https://sallyridescience.ucsd.edu/home/

Index

About the Author

Elizabeth Raum has written over 100 books for young readers. Many are biographies. She enjoys learning about people who help us see the world in new and exciting ways. She lives in Fargo, North Dakota. To learn more, visit her website: www.ElizabethRaumBooks.com.